Farmhouse Christmas

Farmhouse Christmas

Make Your Home a Cozy Haven of Rustic Holiday Charm

KRISTINE STARK

Creator of Farmhouse Green

Foreword by Megan Brokman

Skyhorse Publishing

Copyright © 2025 by Kristine Stark

Foreword copyright © 2025 by Megan Brokman

All rights reserved. No part of this book may be reproduced in any manner without the express written consent of the publisher, except in the case of brief excerpts in critical reviews or articles. All inquiries should be addressed to Skyhorse Publishing, 307 West 36th Street, 11th Floor, New York, NY 10018.

Skyhorse Publishing books may be purchased in bulk at special discounts for sales promotion, corporate gifts, fund-raising, or educational purposes. Special editions can also be created to specifications. For details, contact the Special Sales Department, Skyhorse Publishing, 307 West 36th Street, 11th Floor, New York, NY 10018 or info@skyhorsepublishing.com.

Skyhorse® and Skyhorse Publishing® are registered trademarks of Skyhorse Publishing, Inc.®, a Delaware corporation.

Visit our website at www.skyhorsepublishing.com.

10 9 8 7 6 5 4 3 2 1

Library of Congress Cataloging-in-Publication Data is available on file.

Interior design and layout by Chris Schultz
Cover design by Kai Texel
Cover photos by Kristine Stark

Print ISBN: 978-1-5107-8388-1
Ebook ISBN: 978-1-5107-8473-4

Printed in China

CONTENTS

FOREWORD VII

INTRODUCTION 1

CHAPTER 1 11
Farmhouse Christmas

CHAPTER 2 17
Christmas Home Tour

CHAPTER 3 33
Farmhouse Green

CHAPTER 4 47
Comfort and Joy

CHAPTER 5 57
Winter Solstice

CHAPTER 6 69
Moody Blues

CHAPTER 7 81
French Country Inspiration

CHAPTER 8 91
Classic Red

CHAPTER 9 103
White Christmas

CHAPTER 10 115
The Things We Collect

CHAPTER 11 127
Antiques for Christmas

CHAPTER 12 137
Country Roads

ACKNOWLEDGMENTS 151

FOREWORD

Some people are just naturals, a natural at every single thing they set their heart and mind to, and Kristine Stark is one of those people. Kristine is a natural when it comes to motherhood, friendship, connecting with people on a personal level, decorating, creating a beautiful and welcoming home, photography, styling, finding and capturing the simple beauty in things that are worn and loved, teaching others, and so generously sharing her joy and giving love and wisdom to all she meets.

One of Kristine's many gifts is her ability to so effortlessly place things together and then photograph and capture the beauty she sees in a way that allows the viewer to see it exactly as she sees it, a raw and beautiful complementary collection of things that are tattered, worn, loved, and that all have a story. I met Kristine around ten years ago at the Springfield Antique Show in Springfield, Ohio. I had grown to love her timeless styling and gorgeous photography that graced her Instagram page, but I did not know what the woman behind the scenes creating all that beauty looked like. While we were standing in a line she introduced herself to me as "Farmhouse Green," her Instagram name that she is so famously known for. As everyone does that meets her, I immediately felt at ease with Kristine and loved her gentle and kind nature and her big smile. Kristine and I quickly learned that we both share a passion for family life, being out in nature, for old buildings and antiques, and for finding the beauty in the simple things, and we have been best friends ever since that day. She has been the most wonderful friend to me, and I cannot imagine my life without her.

Kristine and I both sell antiques, and we both love to hunt for one-of-a-kind treasures and to learn the story of the antiques we come across in our work. We also both love to save what many consider garbage . . . for example, those chipped, cracked, and heavily crazed dishes that have been used for so many years and hold the most wonderful stories.

One of the things that I have grown to love and admire the most about Kristine is the care and love she pours into every person and thing in her life. Her attention to detail is unmatched, and she dedicates 100 percent of herself to whatever it is she is working on. Her stunning holiday ideas and photography in this book are a testament to that. Just as I know in my heart that Kristine and I were meant to be a part of each other's lives, I know that her magnificent work is meant to be out in the world for people to see, appreciate, and gain inspiration from. What a gift this book is; now there is a way for all of us to be able to look at and revisit again and again the beauty that Kristine so naturally creates.

—Megan Brokman, @Farmhouse5540

INTRODUCTION

I have enjoyed decorating our farmhouse in Ohio for Christmas more than any other home. It reminds me of a Norman Rockwell home straight out of his *Saturday Evening Post* illustrations. It doesn't need much to spruce her up for Christmas—fresh greenery, extra lights around the home and porch, and some wonderful antique pieces that tell our story.

"Home is the nicest word there is."
—Laura Ingalls Wilder

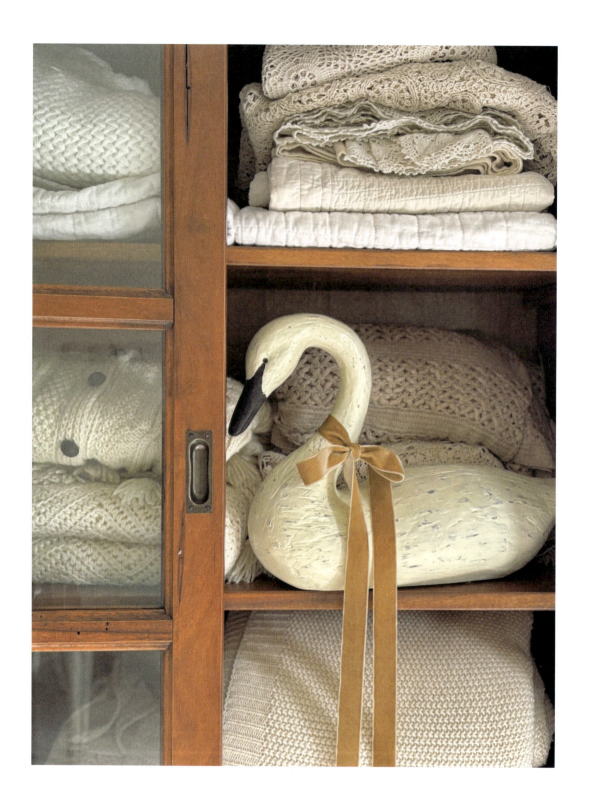

My favorite part of Christmas in this home is knowing that my kids have happy memories of growing up here. They cherish the traditions and experience of Christmas each year in this house. When my kids were young, we often traveled to other places to spend Christmas with family. When we moved to Ohio, we didn't have any of our family close by. It wasn't the tree, the lights, or the decorations that had them smitten—it is the place called "home."

I'm often asked, "How do you do what you do?" Let me encourage you with some simple steps. Be you. Home is the place for you and your family no matter the phase of life you are in. Whether you live alone or have young kids or animals, live in a forever home or a rental, home starts in the heart with you and your family and friends.

Do what you do best, use your strengths, and allow others to gift you with their strengths. I love making my home cozy and comfortable and ready for guests. I do not enjoy baking, cooking, or hosting large dinners. I love meeting people who bake and cook and host meals; these people are a gift to me. Our neighbor makes us homemade rum cakes each year, and I love them all the more because I would never make them myself!

I like to be present and intentional during the holidays. I love my quality time with friends and family at Christmas. My husband enjoys cooking for the holidays, and so do my other siblings and family members. I am thankful for their abilities. I encourage you to simplify at Christmas; use your strengths and let the rest go.

Start small at Christmas when decorating. It is already a busy time, and calendars fill up quickly. Put the big important dates on the calendar and then learn to say no to anything that creates stress instead of joy. Find small places in your home to decorate and, if you like, get the family involved. I start looking for wreaths for the outdoor spaces, we usually get our tree together as a family, and my husband puts up lights. Decorate with the things you love. Tell your story. Do not worry about trends or about how your home compares to others you see in your neighborhood or online.

Comparing to others brings dissatisfaction, but it's wonderful to glean inspiration from other people! I still enjoy looking at magazines, I love Pinterest, and Instagram is full of inspiration. Give credit where credit is due, but there is nothing new under the sun.

"What has been will be again, what has been done will be done again; there is nothing new under the sun."
—Ecclesiastes 1:9

When I started planning for this book, I knew that I could create fun pictures for inspiration, but I felt like every piece of advice had already been given. Then I remembered to do what I do best. I love to take pictures, and I hope that I have encouraged you by doing just that. I hope you find inspiration as you decorate your own home for the holidays!

CHAPTER 1

FARMHOUSE CHRISTMAS

What an honor to get to share beauty with you this season. It has become a quest of mine to capture the hidden beauty in the midst of a very busy season. The Christmas season wraps up a year of experiences and is a wonderful time for reflection. It's also often full of gatherings and events, celebrations with family and friends, and joyful times. It can sometimes be overwhelming. As the end of the year rapidly approaches, I hope you take time to be still and find beauty around you.

FARMHOUSE CHRISTMAS 13

Weathered barn wood with fresh greens—timeless beauty

    Decorating for Christmas is something I look forward to every year. Each home has its own story and traditions, and people have their own motivations for decorating the way they do. I would encourage you to tell your story. I hope to present simple ways to add charm to your home without getting overwhelmed. I pray that these pictures inspire and encourage you to experience hope and peace so that you can prepare your own home for the true meaning of Christmas.

    When I began thinking about writing this book, I kept returning to the spirit of Christmas. This spirit is a deep feeling of comfort, joy, peace, and hope as the year ends. It is the anticipation of being with loved ones and enjoying the final moments of the year together. It also floods my mind with all the Christmas memories over my lifetime and the joy that I have experienced each and every year during this season.

Our Farmhouse Green home

CHAPTER 2

CHRISTMAS HOME TOUR

Last Christmas we had the opportunity to have our home be part of the Christmas in the Village home tour. We have always felt like curators of our old house. In fact, two of the previous owners still live in our small town. It was such an honor to get to share our home with people for the holiday season.

Simple red bench with wreath

Storage shed we love to decorate for the holidays

Preparing our home for an open house seemed intimidating at first, but I liked the idea of it; I have always been one of those curious romantics who longs to see inside every historic home. It was an honor for our home to be on the Christmas tour. Thinking about the people who built the house over a hundred years ago, and all the families that have lived in it since, humbled me. I knew that just as we had fallen in love with this home, so would everyone else who walked through the doors.

I had shared little glimpses of our old farmhouse on Instagram, but it was a different challenge for me to share the historic charm in person. Lucky for us, the tour was only downstairs. People entered from the porch into the living room, then meandered through the dining room, getting glimpses of the stairs, kitchen, and mudroom on the way out the back door to the yard. As I watched strangers appreciate our home, I was reminded of the intrigue and love for all the details that captured our hearts when we bought the house twelve years prior.

It was such a joy to share our home and hear all the comments and praise from visitors. They raved about how we had maintained the old house look, something I treasure. They also complimented us on the carefully planned updates we had done—mostly paint to add to the character of the home and make it our own, and storage in the mudroom for convenience. The greatest compliment came from the owners before us, who said that it looked like the updates had always been there. They appreciated each detail. We have been blessed by every update that the three previous homeowners made, including a mudroom, bathroom, and laundry space with beautiful windows looking out back. Heat and air-conditioning were also updated before we moved in. French doors were added to the dining room to access the patio. We were also told our original, very steep stairs, had been moved from the living room to the dining room to accommodate the family. It is fun to think about how long we will be in this home before the story will continue with another family.

Our porch is the grand entrance to our home, and it is the first thing I transform each season. I prefer fresh wreaths because I don't have the space to store seasonal décor. I have found that local garden stores and big box shops have some good deals on basic greenery for the holidays. Prices change year to year, and I search for the best prices for simple greens. I have also met wonderful friends who have their own local farms. My incredible friend Les handmade all of my fresh garland for my picket fence for our Christmas home show. What a priceless gift. I buy my own simple ribbon to add to the wreaths and greenery. It is easy and satisfying.

CHRISTMAS HOME TOUR

I also search garage sales, estate sales, and flea markets all year long for wreaths that are highly discounted—I keep a few in my limited storage space, but mostly I buy them to resell. Christmas décor is incredibly cheap when bought out of season. I love going to estate sales to find wonderful old things and unique items that aren't sold in stores anymore.

I am notorious for finding free or very cheap furniture for the porch. You can often find timeworn pieces left with the trash on the curb—rustic chairs or small tables make the perfect country scene on the porch or patio, especially with a wreath or some fresh-cut greens propped on them.

When preparing and thinking about how to present our home for Christmas, there were a few things I kept in mind. We live in a hundred-year-old farmhouse, and I love antiques. I wanted to pay special attention to the details of the home that were old, and also show how you can enjoy decorating with simple, practical items that we use daily.

We are fortunate to have the original wood floors and trim, large windows, a built-in china cabinet in our dining room, and a claw-foot tub upstairs for *all* the farmhouse charm. These details are all things I like to highlight in decorating our home. On the other hand, our house lacks large closets and storage space, as well as an oversized garage. There is no basement, just a small crawl space for utilities. When we chose the sweet front porch and humble home to raise our kids and grow old in, we knew we were sacrificing storage space and that we'd have to keep our belongings minimal. It was the right choice. We love our old house with its layers of wallpaper upstairs and its old, chipping deep blue-green paint. It is full of character and just right for our family.

The entrance to your home, front stoop, stairs, or a mudroom can be a great place to start decorating for Christmas. I like to organize our space with baskets and hooks and put away anything extra. I always use what I have on hand first. Take note of all the Christmas items you have stored up before you go looking for anything new. I love to use blankets and sweaters and boots, gloves, and hats that we actually wear to decorate as well. My favorite way to decorate is by using things that are useful and beautiful. I take my cues from my "hygge" friends of Denmark with their cozy but minimalist approach to decorating. One of my absolute favorite books is *The Little Book of Hygge: Danish Secrets to Happy Living* by Meik Wiking. I love his advice for living and for creating a cozy home.

When you know the space you are decorating intimately, you learn to pay attention to the things you bring home, choosing them carefully and with purpose. If you know what you already have, what spaces you want to fill, and the feeling you want to create, collections come together organically.

CHRISTMAS HOME TOUR

Wallpaper in the master bedroom I love and never changed

CHRISTMAS HOME TOUR

This room serves as my office now, but it used to be one of the children's bedrooms. The beautiful wallpaper was here when we bought the place and I'll never change it!

CHRISTMAS HOME TOUR 29

CHAPTER 3

FARMHOUSE GREEN

When I picked up my camera and began to take photos for the first time, I found that capturing beauty gave me the gift of time standing still. Looking over photographs each year had me reminiscing about how incredibly beautiful each season truly was. I had never lived anywhere with such perfectly timed seasons.

Taking pictures to find beauty also turned into taking pictures to stage and sell antiques in my Etsy shop, Farmhouse Green. I have had my Etsy shop for more than twelve years. My favorite thing to sell when I started my shop was antique ironstone dishes and transferware of any color. Ironstone mixing bowls, square bowls, butter pats, and pitchers were top sellers. Transferware in rare colors such as turquoise, green, gray, black, and purple is always fun to find, and brown transferware and transferware with floral designs have always been classics. I sold white linens, quilts, hankies, doilies, and anything crocheted or embroidered. I also loved selling architectural salvage and art that would accent my style. I enjoy hunting for unique treasures, but I don't have the room in my house to hang on to these beautiful things, so it's a pleasure to sell them. I am able to take all my pictures for my shop in my home and share how I would use the items.

Instagram makes it especially easy to connect with people all over the world who share common interests. I find other farmhouse lovers, old house fanatics like me, and antique sellers, collectors, and flea market shoppers as well. Since moving to Ohio, often the places I shop do not have websites or advertising. I find myself in shops with an abundance of incredible antiques and the best prices. It's a dream come true for me. Through Instagram, I share my backroad adventures and advertise for shops along the way. It helps to connect the right people to the right places. I have met so many incredible shop owners and sellers, and I treasure these friends.

I learned to ship dishes while working for Villeroy & Boch when my husband and I lived in Germany. Shipping came naturally to me, and I decided early on that I wanted my antique and vintage items to arrive packed with care and beauty. Part of my love of shipping was wrapping each item as a gift for my customers. I have always had an obsession with pretty paper, ribbon, and stationery and hand-written notes. This became a creative outlet for me, and it was a reasonable way to elevate my shop. I absolutely loved wrapping each item and praying that it would bring a huge smile to my customers on the other end.

It worked, and I have made so many cherished friends and supporters of my shop. Each one of my supporters has their own collections. I often think of my longtime supporters while I am shopping. The highlight of being a shop owner is hearing back from my delighted new or old customers that the items are just as they dreamed, better than the pictures, and that they will treasure them for years to come.

FARMHOUSE GREEN

The gift of connecting with people near and far and building friendships has been the greatest joy, but I also love learning to do new things like staging and photography. I began to create and enjoy this new routine. I learned to shop for specific items and continue to wrap these gifts for my customers.

While setting up my shop for Etsy all those years ago, I did a search on Etsy for shops with the name "farmhouse." I followed all the wonderful shops to learn from them and ask questions. One of those shops was Megan, @Farmhouse5540 in Pennsylvania. I later saw her at the Springfield Extravaganza flea market, where I ran to her booth to buy up all of her "dirty dishes," distressed ironstone, and transferware. Her family was there supporting her along the way. I just loved how they worked together in her booth, which perfectly displayed antique, useful, beautiful things.

It wasn't until a few years later that I actually got the courage to introduce myself. Our relationship grew from seeing each other once or twice a year to not knowing how we would live without each other. We share common interests, hobbies, and values. She is my "farmhouse twin," and when we are together we often get asked if we are sisters. She has introduced me to a world of other shop owners, vendors, and people along the way. What a gift.

Ironstone pitchers and butter pats

Stack of sweaters and cozy blankets ready to use

CHAPTER 4
COMFORT AND JOY

If I had two words to describe my style, they would be "comfort" and "joy." As a young mom raising my kids, I enjoyed keeping things organized and comfortable, but I also liked to find things that brought a smile to my face. It didn't have to be anything big or expensive. I found myself buying things that were utilitarian and came with a story. My mom taught me that quality time with your kids is the greatest gift you can give your children, and I have found that my kids are my greatest treasures. I didn't work outside the home for many years and loved being thrifty. My mom and mother-in-law gifted me with so many things from their homes and bought me things they knew I would love.

Christmas tree in an old crock next to beautiful linens

My mother-in-law had the greatest influence on my style and decorating choices. I cherished my time with her, poring over magazines and dreaming about the homes we would decorate. She taught me to buy old, vintage, and antique items that had a history. She had collected so many beautiful things over the years, and each one came with its own unique place of origin and a story that delighted me each time. She taught me everything there is to know about collecting. She has always been a wise collector, thrifty and with wonderful collections. I like to refer to her as a keeper of all the beautiful things, while I am a seller of all things. We make a good team.

When decorating your home for Christmas, choose things that delight you and tell your story. We have often lived in cold places, and I love to collect sweaters. I display stacks of my sweaters because they remind me of the places we have traveled, and they look beautiful. Your home will always be an evolving story of the places you have been. Each year of living brings new chapters.

Some of the first things I sold in my Etsy shop were natural-colored linens that came in various shades of cream, ivory, or white because I was able to use them in any room. They are easy to mix and match with regular bedding. I use them on couches and our reading chairs to add warmth during the cold winter months. They look beautiful stacked in a cupboard when winter has passed. I found that there were often cheaper than buying new. I bought quilts, coverlets, bedspreads—anything with a beautiful texture or pattern. Handmade blankets, crocheted doilies, runners, and popcorn coverlets were among my favorites. They just shouted "farmhouse" to me.

I opened my Etsy shop the year after we moved into our farmhouse. I wasn't in a rush to make decorating decisions and I couldn't bring myself to remove any of the wallpaper because I was in love with the vibrant floral wallpapers throughout. Buying neutrals helped unify the rooms. If I chose to paint or change up the look of our farmhouse, these blankets and basics would continue to be useful and beautiful no matter the room they were stored in. That is how my love affair with linens started, and they are still my favorite things to collect today.

The things I kept in my home were useful and beautiful, but when it came to things I planned to sell, I enjoyed more creativity and variety. Using inspiration from my wallpaper and painted floors and the colors I found in the barns around town, I craved vibrant colors. I found these in transferware, Currier and Ives tins, and other small items that brought life to my home for a season before being sold.

Pale pink barn with snowy details / Variety of handmade stockings / Chunky ironstone plate with a crocheted snowflake

COMFORT AND JOY

Simple chair and table with a small tree and a favorite antique watercolor set a peaceful scene.

CHAPTER 5
WINTER SOLSTICE

Germany is credited with bringing the Tannenbaum, or Christmas tree, to homes as early as the 1600s, although some point to how early celebrators of winter solstice used fresh greens in their homes over doorways and entrances to ward off evil spirits. Either way, I think we might all agree that the tree is one of the most iconic Christmas traditions today.

Mini crock with spruce branch

WINTER SOLSTICE

Having been born in Germany myself, I love the history and traditions that come from that part of the world. I cherished the time I lived there with my siblings taking hikes, seeing castles, and adventuring. The small towns and Christmas markets were a playground for us as kids. My grandparents would visit and let us know how lucky we were to get to be in such incredible places with our parents.

It wasn't until I married my husband and returned to Germany for three years that I saw how amazing the experience of living there really was. My husband and I spent weekends shopping flea markets and enjoyed food and local restaurants. We were young and not collectors yet, but we took note of all the beautiful things. We bought a few pieces of furniture that we still treasure today. Those years impacted the things we do collect today. We especially loved the slower life and simpler lifestyle.

Wherever you live, get outside and take in the world around you. There is nothing like nature to teach you about change and how to adapt to each season.

There were many years my family would travel to Arizona for Christmas to join my grandparents for their tradition of local fresh tamales and Mexican food on Christmas Eve. This is a tradition my siblings and I have carried on with each of our own families. Many Christmas Eves, we've found ourselves looking up into the desert sky full of stars with cactus all around us. These are Christmas memories I cherish. We always attended Christmas Eve service with my grandparents in Arizona, or whatever part of the world we were living in at the time. We continue this tradition today.

I am not a minimalist by nature, but having a larger family and smaller spaces to store stuff has made me conscious of how much I want to bring into our home. Just as I prepare the outside of our home for winter, I do the same on the inside. I love bringing extra light into the home for Christmas and creating cozy spots designed for sharing a warm meal together or cuddling under blankets. Fresh greens and other natural decorations are ideal for us because they come in from outside and go back out at the end of the season—no storage needed!

There is so much beauty found in the natural world around us. Fall is my favorite season, and after watching it explode in color I am always ready for the muted colors of winter. Over the years my kids and I have enjoyed collecting acorns and pine cones and all things nature to use in our home for the holidays. Taking our cue from the squirrels, we store up the last seeds of fall and lean into winter.

Creels with their natural fibers are fun to fill with greens and spools of ribbon.

When planning for the holidays, walk through your home and see what spaces are easiest to decorate and will be most visible to your family and guests. Take note of your favorite spots to linger with family and decide how you can add Christmas cheer to these spaces. It can be as simple as a collection of blankets, displaying your hats, scarves, and shoes, or adding simple greenery to an entrance. One of the easiest ways to make your home feel festive for the holidays is adding natural-looking greenery to each room. If you don't have access to fresh greens and you have storage space for faux, go ahead and use that—you can hardly tell the difference these days.

I like to decorate with things that will stay with me for a season, long past Christmas day. Lights, greenery, simple organized areas that continue to work hard after the trees have come down—these are my specialty. I also love to decorate smaller trees in different styles and place them throughout the house, giving each room a unique feel.

Natural wood ornaments arranged with wooden beaded garland / Ironstone platter with wood star ornaments

Create a simple vignette using warm-colored baskets and greens. Tie it together with a ribbon to catch your eye.

Sweaters stack for a cozy, organized look in any room.

Currier and Ives prints take you back in time to "the simple life."

FARMHOUSE CHRISTMAS

CHAPTER 6

MOODY BLUES

I love color. It doesn't have to be bold or overbearing, but color is a wonderful way to change the season or mood of a room utilizing smaller interchangeable accessories.

Wood cabinet with antique dishes

MOODY BLUES 71

Growing up, I often found myself in homes with painted walls, carpeting, or rooms with features I could not change for one reason or another. I loved the challenge of making that space my own. I learned the saying "Use it up, wear it out, make do, or do without" from my grandma early on, and it has become one of my favorite mantras. It has served me well.

MOODY BLUES

MOODY BLUES 77

When budgets were tight and we couldn't change certain core features of a room, I just decorated around it. If it's not broken, don't fix it. We waited many years to make changes to our farmhouse. When everyone else was leaning into the simple white farmhouse, which I adored, we waited and embraced our floral wallpaper and butter yellow sponge-painted walls. Our girls often shared rooms, and my son endured the floral wallpaper as a toddler.

I found the Currier and Ives prints one summer, and they captured my heart. A print of a cozy cabin in the woods with a warm fire crackling inside reminded me of the many times we visited my grandparents' cabin in the White Mountains of Arizona as kids. I can only imagine a place like *Skating Scene—Moonlight* (1868). Currier and Ives prints capture beauty and comfort from time past. I find these little prints help me to reflect on the simple things in life. I have sold so many of these over the years, and I just can't seem to leave them behind when I find them.

To create the little scene on the previous page, I used the Currier and Ives print to set the mood against a beautiful antique cabinet. Blue transferware dating back to the 1800s and small clippings of greenery were used to create a natural vignette for the home.

When preparing your home, find things that bring you great joy. Pieces that tell the stories of your past and the collections you have treasured over the years will bring inspiration to those you share them with. It doesn't take much to turn your favorite collections into a little Christmas display; I simply add some fresh greens and maybe some ribbon. Find little Christmas details to finish the look. Your area will be transformed quickly without having to redecorate the space.

While having dinner at my mother-in-law's house, I saw her blue cabinet and knew I had to use it for the book. She reminded me of her antique transferware she had stashed. These were the first pictures I took, and my favorite presentation of Christmas. I believe it captures the spirit of Christmas and the old-house charm.

CHAPTER 7

FRENCH COUNTRY INSPIRATION

I bought my first set of dishes from Villeroy & Boch after three years of working for the company in Germany. My wisdom said to buy something white that would work for every season, but I had fallen in love with the whimsical floral print of the pattern "Vieux Luxembourg." It is said the pattern dates back to 1748. I still use these beautiful dishes every day.

My first collection of dishes was in the Villeroy & Boch Vieux Luxembourg pattern.

French country style is an easy one to include at Christmas. The French are wise in prioritizing the good things in life. They practice slower living, lingering meals with family and friends, and great food and drink. If you already have collections of French country style, make them festive by adding simple elegance with a ribbon, fresh greens, or a beautiful stocking.

FRENCH COUNTRY INSPIRATION

Stacked white linens with a stocking / Architectural trim adds character to the home. / Classic scalloped pedestal ironstone filled with greens and a pine cone

FRENCH COUNTRY INSPIRATION   87

Window with glass bottle collection on display at the Hotel Gallery, Tipp City, Ohio. / Rustic wire basket with wreath and snow / Terra-cotta pots waiting for spring plants

FRENCH COUNTRY INSPIRATION

Vintage Christmas star quilt in wood soda crate with a berry wreath

CHAPTER 8

CLASSIC RED

Is there anything as classic as red décor to bring holiday cheer to your home? From Santa Claus to Martha Stewart, there is a good case to be made that red is the color of Christmas. In Ohio, we see the red cardinals nestled in the trees and bushes. Red rustic barns are abundant, and you can find natural red berries on trees and bushes on a long winter's hike.

CLASSIC RED 93

My mother-in-law introduced me to Martha Stewart early on. We bought up every *Martha Stewart Wedding* magazine we could find while planning my wedding. I loved Martha's elegant but simple style, and her perfectly captured details. We learned so much from Martha Stewart and all of her incredible collections, and of course her organization for everything home-related. She is one of the greatest home decorators, and there isn't anything she doesn't do.

When I sat down to write *Farmhouse Christmas*, Megan handed me a stack of Martha Stewart Christmas books. I didn't even know the books existed. They are filled with absolutely stunning pictures and inspiration, of course, but what shocked me is how timeless they are. They present classic decorating tips that are as beautiful today as they were when the books were written. Some were almost twenty-five years old. The writing, the pictures, the recipes, and style still inspire me.

I have never talked to anyone as knowledgeable about so many kinds of antique collections as my mother-in-law. She loves to read and is the best researcher. I've learned a wealth of information from her and if I ever have a question, she finds an answer. We enjoy visiting estate sales, antique shops, and markets to fill my Etsy shop.

Vintage Christmas collections are often found discounted at estate sales and barn sales. I love all colors, but red is a classic. I keep my eye out for anything unique to fill the spaces in our antique dining room display cabinet. The cabinet has glass doors on the top and extends to our ceiling. It is perfect for Christmas. The bottom has a white cabinet door where I store extra dishes, linens, and candles.

Hand-painted dishes from Ohio's own Cambridge Pottery are among my favorite finds. I have found bowls, plates, and accessories over the years. It is fun to find items that were made in your home state.

CLASSIC RED 95

CLASSIC RED 97

I have known friends over the years who collect postcards, and I love the details. In the past, however, they were pricey. I have enjoyed finding antique postcards in bundles that are much more affordable. It is intriguing to read the beautiful handwritten notes and holiday wishes. When you can find them for a good price, it is exciting.

This might be the time to share that I have a small obsession with ribbon in general, and velvet ribbon is my favorite. Adding ribbon is one of the easiest ways to add a touch of elegance to your home. This is nothing new, of course—just a tool I recommend. I use ribbon on the wreaths, to hang ornaments, and as tiebacks for curtains. I add ribbon to baskets to change them up for the season. It is an easy way to decorate on a small budget, particularly if you buy your ribbon from thrift stores or shop the postholiday sales at craft stores. Ribbon catches the eye, and it is simple and not overdone.

Finding a vintage or antique quilt is the ultimate Christmas treasure. You can use any color quilt; it is becoming harder to find classic red quilts for the holidays. Quilts can be used in any room. I love folded quilts in stacks, or draped over the couch. I use them on my kids' beds with Christmas sheets. It is fun and festive if you are lucky enough to find a red one.

Christmas tableware is another way to add charm to your home and share your collections with others. I am always keeping my eye out for unique patterns. This year I found a Homer Laughlin plate made for a Women's Relief Corps convention probably dating back to the late 1800s. I love to layer colored transferware and ironstone for each season. The options are endless, and it is a joy to search for something unique and red for the holidays.

There are so many other ways to add a little red to your holiday décor. In winter, I search for plants that are in season. The poinsettias are great if you have a warm sunny spot inside for them. This year I found amaryllis blooming at Tractor Supply and quickly bought a few to decorate with. Red carnations, roses, daisies, and so many others can be mixed in with berries and holly, and the options are endless. Tie everything together with a simple ribbon and you will be ready to host friends and family.

CLASSIC RED

CHAPTER 9
WHITE CHRISTMAS

When I worked for Villeroy & Boch while my husband and I lived in Germany, my manager gave me some good advice. She said if you are going to buy an expensive set of dishware, buy white or neutral. She went on to explain that most people only use white china for the holidays, but it is easier to change the tablecloth and accessories each season than it is a whole set of dishes. Although I didn't buy white dishes, I have used this advice as a general guide for decorating. When buying larger items or more expensive items, I go with a neutral, then add all the colorful details—pillows, baskets, curtains, and other accessories.

Collection of handmade white stockings

Ironstone, of course, was a top seller when I started my Etsy shop. My mother-in-law was well ahead of me in the ironstone game and inspired me to collect my own. I found that the "dirtier" and distressed pieces that appeared to be damaged and tea-stained were sometimes tossed aside or highly discounted. I loved these pieces because they showed so much character, and I didn't have to worry about breaking or damaging them because they were already distressed.

I had never seen ironstone before I moved to Ohio. I don't know if I wasn't looking for it, or it all just ended up in Ohio. I learned really quickly to flip it over and look for the manufacturers' stamps. I found ironstone in our local shops and stacked in boxes at flea markets and farm sales.

One time I was shopping in a small-town shop and I picked up a "tea-stained" distressed piece of ironstone. The owner was from England and knew the value of clean, white, pristine ironstone. She pointed to a box in the back room and said, "I have a box of that dirty ironstone in the back I was going to throw out." My heart leapt out of my chest. I quickly said, "I would love to take a look!" I bought the entire box for a few dollars. For many years I didn't have any competition buying "dirty," distressed ironstone. I always saw it as flawlessly aged to perfection.

Snowflake and bells with greenery

I was surprised that I was finding old quilts when we moved to Ohio. They reminded me of the ones my mom had made when she learned to quilt. I would come across old, tattered quilts gently used and passed from generation to generation. The older the better, because I found that the more tattered and worn the edges, the softer they became, and often they were more affordable. I always wash my quilts on a gentle cycle and gently dry. They wash up beautifully and are the softest blankets in the world. They tell a story with every pattern you find.

Trends change, and there was a time, before my time, that antiques were incredibly expensive, and people were trained experts in collecting. Thank goodness I started collecting when antique shoppers were looking for something they could use to tell a story in their home and the more "distressed" and damaged, the better the story. I became affectionately known as "the dirty ironstone girl."

One of the greatest gifts I received after moving into our old farmhouse was a quilt from my mother-in-law. While we were living in Germany, my grandmother passed away in Arizona. My mother-in-law, my fellow treasure hunter and antique lover, went to the estate sale at my grandma's house and bought everything she thought I might like. I was newly married at the time and not a collector yet. We lived frugally and I would rather spend money on travel than buy things I didn't have a place for.

She held on to that quilt until I turned thirty-three and then gave it to me when we moved into our farmhouse. She later shared with me the information given to her about the quilt. It is a white-on-white antique wedding quilt from Denmark. My great-grandmother's family passed it down to each of the daughters in the family. It has white initials for the bride and groom. It has also been rumored that my grandmother came from Danish royalty. It is one of my most treasured possessions. My mother-in-law told me that when you turn thirty, you begin to cherish things from your past and want to start collecting items that have meaning. She was right.

Favorite popcorn crocheted stocking, a gift from my mother-in-law / Stack of quilts on a hope chest with a crock and greens

CHAPTER 10

THE THINGS WE COLLECT

When I am buying home décor, I shop with intention. Will I use the items year-round in some way? The things that I search for are collections that add to my story of home.

THE THINGS WE COLLECT

As I mentioned before, my mother-in-law influenced me to be on the lookout for French classics—bread baskets, scalloped wood salvage, beautiful ornate and embellished linens, and classic art. The French have always been the leaders in style and elegance.

I have many memories and experiences from years of Christmas in Germany. I was born there and so was my youngest sister, Kathleen. My oldest daughter, Sarah, was also born in Germany in the same hospital I was born in. My parents spent many years collecting ornaments at the *Christkindelsmarkts* in Germany. They let us pick out handmade wooden toy ornaments for the tree. Kathleen still collects and treasures these ornaments today.

THE THINGS WE COLLECT   119

Needlepoint Santa pillow / Antique Holland Cocoa tin / Traditional leather lederhosen

My husband and I didn't buy much while living in Germany. We did bring home our beautiful daughter Sarah and incredible experiences of traveling with her all over Europe before she was a year old. She traveled with us to Austria, Switzerland, France, Belgium, and the Netherlands with my mom and mother-in-law when they came to visit. I did buy a tiny set of lederhosen and have pictures of each of my kids wearing them over the years.

We have been blessed to travel to many other places, and each place helped to shape us. My husband spent time in Hawaii while he was in elementary school, and I graduated from high school in Hawaii. We both remember going to the beach on Christmas Day.

The history of our family and experiences plays into the things we collect. Both of our grandfathers' families came from Germany. And because my grandmother's side of the family came from Denmark, I love learning more about their traditions.

Two oil paintings I inherited from my grandma. She brought back postcards of the family's farm in Denmark and had them painted by a neighbor in 1978, the year I was born.

Collection of gold patina, Danish calf, berry tin, oval frame

Sugared fruit / Father Christmas wax ornaments / Danish clock from my grandmother

THE THINGS WE COLLECT   125

CHAPTER 11

ANTIQUES FOR CHRISTMAS

There is a part of me that sometimes wonders if I will ever run out of things to sell or collect. I don't have to search very hard; antiques and treasures seem to find their way to me. When friends and family know you buy and sell antiques, the word gets out. I have been asked to help go through and sort and sell things from the home. This is not something I want to do full-time, but I do enjoy helping others organize, sort, and sell or donate things. I have actually done two estate sales, one for my own home as we were downsizing and one for a friend.

I didn't start out planning to sell antiques and vintage items. I remember my first visit to the Country Living Fair in Columbus, Ohio, like it was yesterday. My mother-in-law had come to visit. My husband drove us and pushed my youngest daughter in a stroller so we could shop this antique haven. I was so excited to see all the incredible booths, vendors, and antiques. I spent the day taking so many pictures because I was in awe of what I saw. I was so overwhelmed by the amount of stuff, I don't think I bought a thing, but it hooked me on antiques.

The next antique show I visited was the Springfield, Ohio, Flea Market at their fairgrounds. My husband and I spent the day getting lost in the endless outdoor and indoor aisles of antiques. I took more pictures, but this time the prices were so low I felt it was my duty to buy. The size of our farmhouse and budget kept me from going into a frenzy, but I could not believe the fairgrounds filled to the brim with every kind of treasure for garage-sale prices. I felt like we had found an untouched gold mine. The flea market was only posted in *Country Living* magazine at the time, and it spread only by word of mouth. There wasn't a website, or pictures, and no Instagram to advertise this show. My husband and I made it our tradition to go every May and September for our anniversary and my birthday. It was only natural for me to open my shop and begin to sell my farmhouse treasures. It was a dream for me to get to find antiques and be able to sell them at bargain prices

to my customers and friends. I shop at this show twice a year with intention to buy for all seasons. I love my local shops in town as well, and Ohio has many wonderful shops and malls to search for treasures.

The rest is history. I have met countless Instagram friends, vendors, buyers, collectors, authors, shop owners, artists, and people from all over the country at the Springfield, Ohio, Flea Market. It is now affectionately referred to as the Springfield Extravaganza. There will always be a deal to be had and something to search for.

ANTIQUES FOR CHRISTMAS

ANTIQUES FOR CHRISTMAS

Some of the most talented vendors, sellers, shoppers, and creative souls set up at Springfield, Ohio. If you don't find everything you need at the flea market, right next door is the Heart of Ohio Antique Center, America's biggest and best antique center with more than eight hundred booths. I don't think I will run out of antiques anytime soon.

As a mom and wife, my family has probably heard me say this phrase more than any other: "People are more important than things." Though I have enjoyed buying, collecting, and selling antique items, nothing compares to the people and friendships I have gained along the way.

My kids were often bribed with ice cream and food to come along with us to Springfield only to find us spending hours talking to the friends, vendors, and people we have met over the years. My son avoids any and all car rides that may be headed to an antique shop or flea market, but each of my girls has learned to love shopping around and finding their own deals. I could probably fill another book with the stories of the Springfield Flea Market. The people I see there are my favorite part.

Springfield Antique Show is a great place to shop for Christmas and a variety of items with vendors coming from all over the country. It is a joy to meet up with friends I have only known or chatted with behind the screen. It is fun to meet in person and be encouraged by each other. Behind every vintage or antique treasure is a person with a story. Though I don't have enough space here, there is a story behind every picture I take.

ANTIQUES FOR CHRISTMAS   135

CHAPTER 12
COUNTRY ROADS

Let us bring more hope, joy, and adoration into our homes and relish in the season as you share your own stories, create your own memories, and celebrate your own traditions at Christmas.

"I swear to you, there are divine things more beautiful than words can tell."
—Walt Whitman

COUNTRY ROADS

I've never owned a camera or learned to use one. I take pictures with my phone. Three years after settling into our farmhouse in Ohio, my kids were off to school, and I had a few extra hours of my own time. I found myself taking pictures on our walks to school and of the daily tasks around the home.

I have always loved cleaning and organizing our home, and when it looked extra clean and pretty, I would snap a picture. Truth be told, I used to be a perfectionist. When I had my children, I learned to let that go. I did have one rule, though: just one room or space had to be neat, clean, and pretty. It allowed the perfectionist deep inside me to feel like I had accomplished some kind of organizational task for the day.

Instagram came out around the same time, and I began to take an interest in photographing displays and vignettes. I enjoyed the comfort and creativity of creating these pictures—it seemed to satisfy my soul. I found myself organizing these pictures neatly by season and color. It was a fun new hobby for me, and took very little time, but gave me a small encouragement and connection with other people. I loved the access to people with similar interests, hobbies, and collections all over the world.

Through Instagram, I have often been asked by my followers and friends to print or sell my photos. I have made small attempts to sell a few cards and some small pictures, but nothing that was feasible. This year after many requests, my sister asked me to think about putting together a "Christmas Farmhouse" book. I was humbled and honored and began to put things together in my head, and then into photos, and lastly, words.

The spirit of Christmas tradition in our home is the celebration of our Savior, Emmanuel, which means "God with us." From the time I was young, our family has read this passage at Christmas:

*For to us a child is born,
to us a son is given,
and the government will be on his shoulders.
And he will be called
Wonderful, Counselor, Mighty God,
Everlasting Father, Prince of Peace*
—Isaiah 9:6

    God never ceases to amaze me with the beauty of His creation and the details and plans for my life. It brings me joy to get to point to Him through the beauty captured through the lens of my phone's camera.

146 FARMHOUSE CHRISTMAS

Every person longs to be seen and known and to find connection. I am honored to share with you the beauty of the season, and point to the Savior, Emmanuel, "God with us."

How do I capture beauty? Most often I find beauty when I have felt alone or lost and needed a guide. I love the quote by C. S. Lewis, "I believe in Christianity as I believe that the sun has risen: not only because I see it, but because by it I see everything else."

I encourage you to search for beauty around you every day, and to take moments to be still. Revel in the beauty of nature, the season, and every good gift that comes from Emmanuel, God with us.

COUNTRY ROADS

ACKNOWLEDGMENTS

I thank God for allowing me to share the beauty of the world around me with everyone I meet. I thank God for using me to point to Him every day I live on this earth.

> "You are the God who sees me," for she said,
> "I have now seen the One who sees me."
> —Genesis 16:13

I thank God for my dad who taught me to read the Bible and find wisdom and encouragement every day.

I thank my mom, who taught me to pray for everyone I meet.

I thank my brother Derek for helping me to put into words who I am and what it is I have done with my life.

I thank my sister Kathleen, who flew me to Toronto to celebrate before I even had a contract with a publisher because she believed in me.

I thank my husband, who has made every dream that I have had come to life. I would be lost without him. He made time for me each and every day. He helped me write every page of this book.

I thank each one of my kids for cheering me on and praying for the whole process and being patient as I wrapped myself up in this work. They allowed me to turn our home into a Christmas display from July through January. My kids are my greatest treasures. They teach and inspire me every day.

This book idea was born when my sister Rebekah asked me to write a book. She came up with the idea, the title, and went to work for me. She walked me through each and every step of the way and matched me with Abigail Gehring from Skyhorse Publishing. Rebekah encouraged me with the phrase, "It only takes one!" It only takes one person to "see" you and want to hear your story. What a journey it has been.

I thank Jevon and Embolden Media Group. Jevon is full of knowledge and life-giving encouragement. She organized my life and carried me through the process of becoming an author. She spends her life sharing tools and equipping new authors to reach their dreams.

I thank Diana and Jerry, my in-laws who opened their home to me to start taking pictures on day one. My mother-in-law Diana taught me everything I know about antiques, Martha Stewart, and home decorating. My in-laws have known me since I was sixteen and have cheered for me every step of the way.

I thank one of our oldest friends, Dale, who booked a trip to the Dominican Republic for us to celebrate in September before I even signed a contract. *Farmhouse Christmas* became available to the world for preorder on Superbowl Sunday, the night we flew to the Dominican Republic. God is good.

I thank every one of my family, friends, and members of my social media community who have prayed this book through. Thank you for this opportunity to point to God!

Merry Christmas!

Photo by Michael S. Stark